THE SILENCE OF SEPARATION

THE SILENCE OF SEPARATION

A Kids Guide to Divorce

Raya

NEW DEGREE PRESS
COPYRIGHT © 2022 RAYA
All rights reserved.

THE SILENCE OF SEPARATION
A Kids Guide to Divorce

ISBN
979-8-88504-401-1   *Paperback*
979-8-88504-265-9   *Kindle Ebook*
979-8-88504-263-5   *Digital Ebook*

For my sister, who is a constant source of inspiration and an incredible sister. For my mom, who helped me with this book and who is the best momma in the whole world. To my dad, who I love very much. To all of my friends, and to Max and Rocco, who are rocking this new hard situation.

CONTENTS

	INTRODUCTION	9
CHAPTER 1	DIVORCE	13
CHAPTER 2	HOW TO FIND YOUR SAFE PERSON	19
CHAPTER 3	WHY LISTENING HELPS	27
CHAPTER 4	USE YOUR VOICE	33
CHAPTER 5	NOT YOUR FAULT	39
CHAPTER 6	THE PHYSICAL SYMPTOMS OF SEPARATION	45
CHAPTER 7	I MISS U	53
CHAPTER 8	A NEW STEP	59
CONCLUSION	A GAME OF LEAPFROG	67
	APPENDIX	69
	ACKNOWLEDGMENTS	71

INTRODUCTION

Are your parents going through a divorce like mine did? It's really hard and not fun. My name is Raya, and I am twelve years old. I chose to write this book because divorce doesn't just affect the parents... it also affects the kids. My parents are divorced, and it is hard—separate houses with different rules and different decorations. Vacations can be weird too. I sometimes saw my parents upset too and that's hard. It just feels different and your life changes so fast. Even things like a different toothbrush at one house can be hard.

As I got older, I realized I wasn't alone, because I made a few friends at school whose parents are also divorced. I realized at that point how many children's parents are divorced. One of my best friends, Mira, has been really helpful because she has two houses and understands that some days are just hard. For whoever is reading this book, if your parents are divorced, I really hope to help you through this difficult process.

I was so little when my parents got divorced that I don't really remember when they told me. But I do remember that we took a vacation to San Diego, and my dad stayed at one hotel while my mom stayed at a separate one. My sister and I switched every day from our mom's hotel to our dad's hotel, and I didn't really know what was going on with my parents. I wasn't really aware that they weren't friends anymore.

It got harder going from one house to the other. It didn't feel fair. Why did I have to move houses but my parents didn't have to move? It feels like parents don't understand because they don't have to jump back and forth from house to house. Once my dad moved to another house, my mom moved into a different house as well. At some point I just got used to moving, but each transition was still hard because I was leaving one parent and going to the other one.

All I knew was the term "separated." Soon, I learned the term "divorced." I didn't fully understand either term. Having two houses now makes school and projects hard because you have to do homework and bring projects from house to house, and then you sometimes forget things, and... let's just say it just gets more stressful.

I just want to let whoever is reading this book—whether your parents live in different states, you have a stepparent, or whatever your situation is—to know that you are *not* alone. Did you know that 50 percent of the children in the US will witness their parents being divorced? Sadly, it is not an uncommon thing. But it is so hard, no matter what situation you're in.

Your parents might have scheduled a therapist or a school counselor to talk to you. They *are* very helpful and have helped me through many things. I am *so grateful* for them. But you can also feel connected and more understood when you talk to a peer or anyone who has gone through this or is going through it with you. That is why I am writing this book. I want kids like you to have these tools to help you even more through this very difficult process. I want to help you on this really difficult path—that you have no control over—and help you feel less alone.

Now, before we get started, I need to say a few things.

One of my favorite stories in this book is when I talk about how meaningful it is to listen to other people during stressful times. For me, I had to learn to be a better listener even when I didn't like the conversation. I also want to note that your parents being divorced is stressful, and you don't need to deny that. It is okay to cry. Crying helps us release our emotions. You should do that instead of holding it in, or else you can get sick. This book will include some tools to help you calm down and become less stressed. I have included a mindfulness activity at the beginning of each chapter that I encourage you to do and maybe share with other people.

Divorce is a heavy topic. It's a great idea to write everything down in a journal. In fact, that would be an amazing idea! I have a few journaling pages in this book, but it would be awesome to ask one of your parents—if you haven't already—to get you a journal you can write in whenever you feel like it. Trust me! It helps.

You can also draw pictures of how you feel at the very moment. If how you feel changes, don't change the whole drawing. Just keep on drawing until you feel you are done. It doesn't matter how good it is. Just draw.

Adults need help through a divorce, but the kids do, too. We need strategies to help us cope with this difficult process. So, this book is for kids whose parents are divorced and who need to find coping strategies.

This book will include some of the hardships of your parents being divorced, such as my story, and hopefully will help guide you through them. This is an activity journal, too! It has tips, stories, journaling, and even mindfulness from trained professionals. I really hope this helps because you have no idea how important it is to have guidance through this process, just like I did, and I want you to benefit from this book.

Life is an adventure that none of us should go through alone, especially during tough times like a divorce. Most of the tough stuff about divorce is in this book, including learning how to live with stepparents, half-siblings, and much more. If what you are going through happens to not be in this book, you can always ask a safe person or friend, and maybe some of the strategies could still help you. This is such a hard thing to go through as a kid... but you are not alone. So many kids out there are in a similar situation as you are. And you have so many ways to cope with it.

1

DIVORCE

It's the moment when your entire world is turned upside down and it feels like nobody understands how you feel. Divorce is a hard thing to go through especially when you are a kid—separate houses, two different rooms, your parents not living together. Basically, everything that used to be your life has changed, and you just have to deal with it because you are just a kid.

It feels like when I have just settled down at one house, I have to move to the other one. And witnessing a fight or an argument between your parents is the worst. It makes me feel like I don't have control over what is happening. Like I just want to teleport somewhere else until it is over.

When my parents got divorced, I was only five, so I don't really remember them telling me about it. I just remember weird family meetings that I didn't understand. However, it was really hard when I had to start going from house to house.

One of my friends, Layla, knows exactly how some of you feel. She says her parents would ask her some questions, like "Where's your home?" and it made her feel like she had to choose between her parents. And they also said bad things about the other parent. Everybody probably has a different way of thinking about these difficult changes, but as Layla says, "It was a whole roller coaster." I can relate to that. But no matter what, she still loves both her parents.

I'm sure you can relate to her story a little bit. Right? If you're feeling pressured to make a decision about what house you want to be at or what parent you like more, remember to do what *you* want, not what your mom or your dad might want you to do. You don't have to choose a side, because that's not your job.

You are not responsible for your parents' emotions, because divorce is hard enough without your parents fighting.

Divorce might make you cry a lot but know that you should **never be ashamed of your tears**. I cry a lot because that is how I release emotions. Some people are different, and that's okay. It's important for you to understand yourself so you can use personal tools to help you through a tough situation.

It helps to remember the happy things because if you change your thoughts, you can change your life. Well, that's what my mom always says. Sometimes, I will just talk to my sister. She is funny and always makes me laugh. We are a good team, and I am very lucky to have her because she is really the only other person who is with me almost all the time and understands this feeling.

If you don't have a funny sister like I do, try to remember a time or a feeling that made you feel happy. Maybe it's the beach or the smell of cookies. Whenever I smell fresh coffee, I think of my mom, and it helps.

A good way to help cope with these feelings is to log how you feel and maybe talk to your safe person, like a friend, about it. You might be wondering what a safe person is. Well, I have an entire chapter about that, but the short version is a person who is one hundred percent there for you. They are safe. You can tell them anything and they will listen.

You might say, *why*? Why does this have to happen to *me*? Even though it might not feel like it, you are *not* alone. So many other kids' parents are divorced. Sadly, it isn't a rare thing. It happens a lot. At least one in two children will experience divorce (Lazic, 2022). That's a lot of kids.

So maybe you could try to find a friend whose parents are also divorced, a teacher, or a therapist... Maybe even a random person at the park! Just remember to stay safe... stranger danger! The point is, your safe person could be anyone! It is *so* much easier to focus on school and fun activities when you know you have someone who understands what you are going through.

But first, try this mindfulness exercise. Mindfulness is a practice that helps people look at their own feelings and change their attitudes. Read below to learn how this activity can help you feel better about your parents' divorce.

MINDFULNESS

1. Create a mindful transition, which can be a simple deep breath that allows you to be in the moment. My mom says it's keeping your head where your feet are.

2. Once you create that transition between your home, your school, and your current feelings, visualize the perfect relaxation spot. Maybe it's your bed, a comfy chair, or a swing outside.

3. Put yourself in a calm and restful happy place to help you move your mind from stress, sadness, homework, or other responsibilities.

Now it's time to figure out your feelings. This is a helpful tool I have used to do that. I do this after a mindfulness exercise because my head is clearer.

Here is a log for how you are feeling! You can take a picture of it, or you can copy this page and print it out again.

Whose house are you currently at?

❑ Mom's
❑ Dad's
❑ _____
❑ _____

Write down how you are feeling at the moment:

_____

Why? _____

Where do you want to be right now?

❑ Mom's house
❑ Dad's house
❑ I am perfectly fine right here
❑ Friend's house
❑ Outside
❑ At school
❑ Other _____

Why?_____

You don't have to, but if you feel like it, reflect on your responses. How are you feeling right now? If you want to share your feelings with a safe person, you might find that really helpful.

_____

_____

_____

_____

_____

_____

_____

_____

It's important to learn how you can manage stressful times with tools. This chapter provided you with two different tools to help. Keep reading and you can learn more.

2

HOW TO FIND YOUR SAFE PERSON

―

No matter if a divorce is not so hard, hard, or really hard, it's important to have a safe person. Here, we will talk about what makes someone a safe person and how to find them. If you already have a safe person to talk to, you don't need to read this, but you are welcome to anyway.

I don't play sports, but once I tried softball. I didn't like it, but I tried it. My dad really wanted me to like softball because he wanted to do something with me and connect. But I looked at butterflies and flowers and dirt instead, and I missed the ball a lot. In fact, one time I got hit in the face with a ball because I was looking at the flowers. It really hurt.

Even though I was scared, hurt, and distracted, all I could hear was my mom and a few other people cheering for me. You know how parents do that and cheer for you even when there isn't anything to cheer about? That's the feeling of having a safe person. They don't really care if you are good at something. They just cheer you on no matter what.

Have you ever had a teacher, a coach, or a friend's parent you feel comfortable with? Do you know someone you really trust, who you know cares about you? Do you know someone who just really wants to know you? That's what I call a "safe person."

Finding a safe person to talk to during stressful times is *really* important. I have many safe people, but I found one of them through one of my teachers! She recommended that I go to this wonderful place called ArtPlay. It is art therapy for kids, and I found one of my safe people there. She is my therapist and helps me a lot. We talk about what is troubling me and how to help it. Talking about what is going on and letting it all out helps *a lot*.

Your safe person doesn't just have to be a therapist. It could be your school counselor, your friend, or maybe even your mom or your dad. But your safe person should be someone you trust. Someone you can talk to with ease and maybe even someone who has some idea of what you are going through.

Talk to this person and know that you are safe and loved. It could be multiple people, even. And, if you need more help, here is a chart to help you.

FINDING YOUR SAFE PERSON
Name of the person: _____

On a scale of one to ten, how much *do* you trust this person?

1 - I trust this person *a lot*.

10 - I don't trust this person at all.

1	2	3	4	5	6	7	8	9	10
❑	❑	❑	❑	❑	❑	❑	❑	❑	❑

If you choose above a six, this person might be someone you should talk to. But the closer to ten, the better. I based the number system on my own thoughts and feelings. You might rate your numbers differently and that's okay.

If you don't have a safe person, you have a few other options. For example, art. Art of all sorts can help you express your feelings. You can journal about how you feel, sing, make music, paint, draw, or whatever helps you express your feelings. You can share this art with your safe person, family, friends, or just keep it to yourself, but never underestimate the power of creativity. It's healing.

Finding a safe person is one of the first things you should do because everyone needs someone who can listen, help, and care about how you are feeling. You can have different safe people in your life too. You just need to know that no matter what you have someone to support you.

MINDFULNESS

My school counselor, Maria Roman, helps me a lot. She is one of my safe people and gave me most of these mindfulness ideas. I will mention her throughout this book because she is really special and helpful.

Imagine yourself walking on a trail in the forest, hearing the sticks and twigs crackling under your feet and smelling the muskiness of the forest. As you walk, notice how you feel. The breeze on your skin and the smell of fresh flowers in your nose. Take as much time as you need here to rest and relax. Once you are here in this restful place, take a moment to remind yourself that you are safe and loved.

After this mindfulness, it might be a good idea to journal about how you feel.

_____

_____

_____

_____

_____

_____

BEING GRATEFUL

Gratitude is very important. Reminding yourself what you are grateful for is a very important mindfulness tool. When you ask yourself, "Why *me*?" it's easy to feel like you don't have a lot to be grateful for. You can feel better by remembering good things, places, or people in your life. It's normal to feel bad during this process. I know it has happened to me. Sometimes when I am stressed about a project or have something due for school, and I have to go to another house, I can feel this way. I have literally said, "Why is this happening to me?" I have used this tool to bring me back to a calm place in my mind. It begins by writing down five things you are grateful for and why are you grateful for them.

1. Here is an example: *I am grateful for my mind and my body.*

_____

Why? *My mind is strong and smart, and I can learn new things. I am grateful for my body because it is healthy and I am not sick.*

_____

_____

_____

2. _____

Why?

_____

_____

_____

_____

3. _____

Why?

_____

_____

_____

_____

4. _____

Why?

_____
_____
_____
_____
_____

5. _____

Why?

_____
_____
_____
_____
_____

3

WHY LISTENING HELPS

Having a strong bond with your parents is important. Even if you are mad at them or don't see them a lot, it is still so important. Sometimes when I get upset, I stop talking and just think about things instead. But that changed after this one meeting at my synagogue's one-hundredth-anniversary event.

Together we were writing a new Torah, which is a big deal in Judaism. Not only do we get a new Torah, but we get to help write in it too! At this event, the Torah scribe told us about the letter we would write in our new Torah.

The letter was a *mem*, and he told us that a *mem* meant to listen to other people and that listening is an act of love. I remember he was looking straight at me, and I had the biggest grin on my face. I felt like he saw me, and he didn't even know me. It was really amazing. He was saying that if you only talk about yourself, the other person might think you had a bad day. But if you do it the next day, they might not feel good. He told us that when you listen, it makes the other person feel respected and loved.

Listening to someone doesn't mean that you have to agree with what they are saying. It just means you are hearing what they are saying. That means not talking over them, not trying to interrupt them with your ideas and thoughts, but listening.

Sometimes when I feel lost, I want to talk to my safe person about something, I tell them what is wrong and ask I can do anything to help it; that helps tremendously. But when they start to give me advice and talk to me about it, they sometimes share their stories of when they were in a similar situation. And that makes me feel even better. It makes me feel less alone, and I am not carrying so much all by myself.

During a divorce, so much is out of your control. Sometimes, I felt like nobody was listening to me. Sometimes, I didn't want to listen to what others were telling me, either. Talking to the Torah scribe helped me understand how important it is to listen to other people even when I don't like what they are saying.

Many adults don't listen to kids like us because we are younger. That can make us angry, and it sometimes makes me angry. When that happens, I use some of these strategies to help.

SQUEEZE AND RELEASE

This exercise helps a lot when you are mad or feel like people don't hear or aren't listening, and you just need to release some stress. For this exercise, you can read this while doing it, because it doesn't require you to close your eyes.

Start by squeezing your feet. Hold it for:

1
2
3
4
5

Now release.

Tense up your legs really tight, and hold for:

1
2
3
4
5

And release.

Now tense up your stomach, and hold for:

    1
    2
    3
    4
    5

And release.

Now tense up your hands, and hold for:

    1
    2
    3
    4
    5

And release.

Tense up your arms, and hold for:

    1
    2
    3
    4
    5

And release.

Now, tense up your face and neck, and hold for:

    1
    2
    3
    4
    5

And release.

Reflect on that exercise. How did that make you feel?

Where do you think you feel the most stress? Try squeezing and releasing that part, and see how it feels afterward.

_____

_____

_____

_____

LISTENING

Listening is so important. This activity hopefully helps you practice listening. And even if you can't hear, you have many other ways to listen. You can listen to body language, or you can listen to art because so many things have emotions that you can listen to and see.

Would you rather listen to…

A. Sports
B. Music
C. Building instructions
D. Other_____

If you choose sports, maybe you could listen to a sports radio. Once the game is over, talk to someone about what happened or write it down and see what you can remember.

If you choose music, try to listen to your favorite song. Once it is over, try to figure out what the artist was trying to tell the listener? Listen closely to the key. Major or minor? Happy or sad melody? And listen to the lyrics (if any). Are there things you don't understand? Do the lyrics mean anything to you?

If you choose to build something, maybe listen to a video where they are building something and then build it. Is building something while just listening to the instructions harder for you? Is it easier to look at something and build it? Why or why not?

If you choose other, try to follow the instructions above and reflect on them.

It's important to listen to other people, but it is even more important to listen to yourself. Remember to tell yourself positive things and listen to your body when you are having a hard time. Listening sounds easy, but it's actually kind of hard. It's okay to feel whatever you are feeling, but try to listen to what is being said too.

I am still learning this principle. For me, I go back to what the scribe told me: If you only talk about yourself and you never listen to anyone else, people might stop listening to you, too. So take the time to listen. It might help.

4

USE YOUR VOICE

Have you tried to say something and felt like nobody heard you? Using your voice is hard, but extremely important. After my parents got divorced, my dad married someone else. They had a baby together, and it was really hard for me.

About a week before my stepmom gave birth, I wanted to ask if I could go to my mom's house instead of somewhere else because I wanted to be with my mom if my stepmom went into labor when we were at my dad's house. I was worried that by asking them to go to my mom's house, I would hurt their feelings or get in trouble.

I practiced what I was going to say so it would be easier to express my feelings. I decided to tell my dad and stepmom my feelings in an email. When I came back to their house, we had a discussion about it, and they said yes! For me finding my voice is something I have been working on. If you don't have a problem with this that's great, but it can be difficult when you have no idea how to do it.

I was worried they would say no, maybe even yes, or that their feelings would get hurt, or I would get in trouble for asking. However, I have learned you have to use your voice if you want to be heard and understood.

Adults should be able to control their emotions, and you shouldn't get in trouble for stating or asking something. But if you are nervous still, and backing down, don't get upset at yourself. It's a pretty hard thing to do. Talk to your safe person for some advice. You could write it down, or even take a video. It's your choice.

FIND YOUR VOICE THROUGH MEDITATION
My school counselor, Ms. Roman, gave me this meditation. This is a love and kindness meditation, called *meta meditation*. If meditation is new to you, that's okay. Read the whole meditation before you start or listen to the recording.

Meditation is a way to slow down your many fast thoughts. My mom said it's like keeping your head where your feet are. It starts by just sitting still.

You don't have to do anything—just sit still and try to relax your body. I think about each part of my body—from the top of my head to the bottom of my feet—relaxing my fingers, toes, arms, and face.

After you are still, take some deep breaths. That can be harder than it sounds. But try to take some deep breaths and blow it out. Try to inhale through your nose to the count of four and exhale loudly from your mouth to the count of four.

Once you're ready, try these steps.

1. Gently close your eyes or look down at the floor.

2. Begin by taking a few deep breaths.

3. Consider a person in life who is easy to care about. It could be a good friend, parent, animal, or person that you care about. Imagine them sitting in front of you and looking into your eyes.

4. Get a sense of your heart, like that warm feeling you have when you're being hugged by someone you love. You can picture your heart smiling inside your body or it becoming a happy red color in this moment. With positive intentions, say to this person in your mind, *"May you be happy. May you be healthy in body and mind. May you be safe and protected from inner and outer harm. May you be free from the fear that keeps you stuck."*

5. Again, keep breathing in and out, connecting with your heart.

6. Now, incline your heart and mind toward yourself and say,

"May I be happy. May I be healthy in body and mind. May I be safe and protected from inner and outer harm. May I be free from the fear that keeps me stuck."

7. Now, think of a person who is problematic. Maybe someone who has hurt your feelings, been unkind to you, or you had an argument with. Say in your mind,

"May you be happy. May you be healthy in body and mind. May you be safe and protected from inner and outer harm. May you be free from the fear that keeps you stuck."

8. Now, think of everyone in the whole universe. Say in your mind,

"May you all be happy. May you all be healthy in body and mind. May you all be safe and protected from inner and outer harm. May you all be free from the fear that keeps you stuck."

Listening and thinking with your heart is so important when you use your voice. When you speak to someone, even if you might be mad, still try to give the person good wishes. Try to reflect on this meditation, and what it means to you.

PRACTICING

Here's what I do if I am a little afraid to ask for help. I write down what I want to say in an email. You could even mail it to them on paper! That way, you can't undo it. It's done, and they can have some time to think about it!

You can practice it right here:

_____

_____

_____

_____

_____

_____

_____

_____

It doesn't have to be long; it just has to be in your own words, and say what you think is right. If you have another strategy or you need help coming up with one, talk to your safe person or write it down in a journal.

Your voice is your best tool. Don't let it go to waste.

5

NOT YOUR FAULT

When my parents first separated, I remember having a meeting on the couch. I think they said a bunch of other stuff, but I don't remember. I just remember them telling me that they loved me, and it wasn't my fault. I didn't really understand what they were saying, because it was just weird, but I remember feeling confused about why we were having this conversation.

Later, when I started to go to separate houses, I thought about ways I could fix my parents' problems. I would see if I could get my mom to come over to my dad's, and I thought if I could just get us all back together again I could fix their marriage. That didn't work. I couldn't fix their marriage. I was upset and cried. I think this was the first time I realized it wasn't my responsibility to fix my parents' problems and feelings.

Now I know the fact my parents weren't friends anymore wasn't my fault, but at the time when it first happened it was hard to understand. I told my safe people and my friends that I wanted to get my parents back together. I remember even working a plan with friends at school to see if they could help me get my parents back together. When I explained what I was doing to my safe person, she told me that I'm a kid, and it isn't my problem to fix after all. They would remind me that the only person that I needed to worry about was me.

In fact, my mom often tells me that my feelings are my biggest gift. If we let other people tell us not to cry or not to laugh or not to feel sad, we will never truly understand our own feelings and that is really sad.

If you thought it was your fault, it is *not*. It is usually because your parents already don't get along too well. So don't blame yourself or try to fix their problems. Blaming it on yourself is only going to hurt you even more. I did that for a little bit but at some point, I realized I couldn't fix it, and it was okay. I learned that my only job was to be myself—learn in school, be a good sister, and have fun with my friends.

HAVENING

My school counselor, Ms. Roman, gave me this mindfulness technique—self-havening. Self-havening can help with phobias, anxieties, stress responses, and many other issues. This exercise is a way to show self-love. Remember it isn't your fault. Remember to read these instructions before trying it out. You can even have your safe person read this to you as you try this exercise.

First, start to clear your mind and begin self-havening by applying a havening touch on the face. You can do this by placing your hands over your face so they are covering your whole face and then moving them outside toward your temples and back in about once per second to the count of twenty.

Then hug yourself and act as if you are giving yourself a hug. Rub your arms up and down like you are trying to warm up from the cold to the count of twenty. Finally, place your hands in a namaste position together in front of you with the palms touch. Rub them back and forth as though you are trying to keep your hands warm to the count of twenty.

While you are doing each of these steps, keep your eyes closed and visualize yourself walking up a flight of stairs. Count out loud from one to twenty with each step. As you climb, imagine yourself becoming calmer and more peaceful. You may still feel stressed but at least you can feel better right now.

If you want to journal about how you feeling after this exercise you can do it here:

_____

_____

_____

_____

_____

_____

_____

WAYS TO HELP YOURSELF FEEL BETTER

Below are three different ways to help if you are feeling like the divorce is your fault. In school, we talk about different learning styles: kinesthetic, auditory, and visual. We all learn differently, so we all heal differently. Try one of these, depending on your learning style.

Kinesthetic learners (learns by doing stuff):

As a Kinesthetic learner, try writing down: *It's not my fault*, or do anything to tell yourself it isn't your fault. You could also act it out, dance it out or use any movement you feel comfortable with to move the feeling out of your body.

Auditory learners (learns by hearing or listening):

As an Auditory learner, try repeating a mantra, like: "It was not my fault. I don't blame myself."

Or, have someone else say: "It was not your fault. Don't blame it on yourself."

You can also record yourself saying that and replay it so you can hear your words.

Visual learners (learns by watching or using images):

Visual learners remember more when they read on their own, see things written out, or use charts or pictures. If you are a visual learner, try drawing it out on a piece of paper. Or if you're good with the computer, draw, type, or read it yourself.

If that doesn't work, try to get your mind off it. Go outside for a walk, play with your friends, your pet, your sibling, or do the mindfulness at the beginning of this chapter!

On the hard days, just remember it's not your fault.

6

THE PHYSICAL SYMPTOMS OF SEPARATION

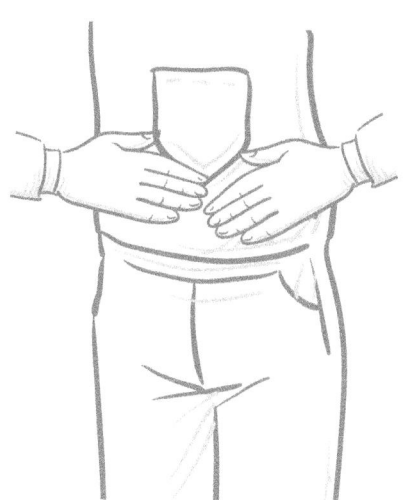

You know that feeling of wanting to be in two places at once? Like if you are invited over to two different friends' houses at the same time? How do you choose? You feel like you are being pulled in two different directions and you don't want to hurt anyone's feelings. You end up feeling badly because whatever you decided to do, you will hurt someone else's feelings? Sometimes you feel this way when you have two houses too. I know I feel this way.

If you feel like you are being pulled between two places, you might experience the following symptoms: constipation, stomachache, etc. These may sound disgusting, but they happen.

I remember when I got appendicitis and how much it hurt. One night, I was setting up a game at my dad's. Suddenly, I felt a small pain like a cramp. The pain got worse and worse, and then I started throwing up. I tried to go to sleep, but after a little while, my dad came into my room and told me that we were going to the hospital.

I looked around the room and saw my sister still sound asleep. I was feeling very nervous. We arrived at the emergency room at Phoenix Children's Hospital. We found out I had appendicitis and that I needed surgery. It was scary, and I didn't like this experience at all. This was during COVID, so the hospital only let one parent at a time, and that made everything even worse. When you go to the hospital it's sometimes scary, but late at night is even scarier.

The doctor and nurses took such good care of me and were so kind. They helped me feel better and less scared. At some point, they let both of my parents in my room and that was so much better. Soon, I had to have surgery, and the nurses and staff brought me soup and card games. I was so touched and moved by how kind they were, despite how busy their jobs are. Soon enough, I was out of the hospital.

One thing I learned from this experience is that your body tells you stuff. Like when your stomach hurts, or head hurts, or going to the bathroom is hard, all of that is your body talking to you. How cool is that? You never feel lonely when you know your body is there to talk to you.

I learned how important it was to listen to my body. Especially when you are going through a hard time. Everything you feel is in your body. So, as important as it is to take care of yourself mentally, you should also take care of yourself physically.

Appendicitis can be caused by repressed (held inside your body) anger (Bourbeau, 2014). Even if you didn't know how you got it, you still have to tell your parents if something is hurting or bothering you. If you *are* experiencing these issues, tell one of your parents.

Ask them to take you to get it checked out because they can be pretty uncomfortable and painful sometimes, and you need to take care of yourself. If you have a younger sibling who doesn't want to read this book, make sure they are okay, too. But focus on you. One of the things that helps me a lot is herbal medicine. Ginger and dandelion root are great healing sources (Gallagher, 2015)!

TAKING A MINDFUL WALK
My school counselor, Ms. Roman, gave me this meditation. This meditation is a mindful walk meditation. Please read the whole meditation before you start. Or, you can listen to the recording.

Start by taking a walk outside. Get some fresh air and sunshine! If you are unable to do that at the moment, take a walk inside your house or in your backyard.

As you are walking, start to notice the following things one by one.

1. Do a body check. Notice how your body feels. Are you feeling heavy or light, stiff or relaxed? Take a few seconds to become aware of your posture and the way you're carrying yourself.

2. Observe. Without trying to change the way you're walking, simply observe your gait. Bring your attention to it. This can sometimes make you feel self-conscious, but that feeling usually passes.

3. Tune in to what is going on around you. Other people, trees, the movement and still of things, or any other sights that come into your awareness field. You're not thinking about any of these things, though; you're simply acknowledging what you see.

4. Note the sounds around you. What can you hear? Again, try to realize any noise but not dwell on it.

5. Notice the smells. Now turn your attention to any smells, whether pleasant or unpleasant. Notice how the mind habitually wants to create a story out of each smell and how it might remind you of somewhere, something, or someone.

6. Physical sensations. How does the weather make you feel? How does it feel as the sole of your feet touch the ground? There's still no need to think about any of these observations. Simply notice, acknowledge, and let go.

7. Focus on your rhythm. Use that rhythm—the soles of the feet touching the ground—as your base of awareness, a place you can mentally come back to when your mind wanders off. Repeat this throughout your walk, step by step.

SELF CHECK-IN

Self-reflecting may not always seem fun, but it is important. If you don't want to, you don't have to, but it just helps you see if your body needs anything from you.

Checking in with yourself daily or weekly can really benefit you. This little check-in is a list of questions to ask yourself. I recommend coming back to this chapter and using the check-in again whenever you feel you need to.

1. How often do you poop?
A. Every day
B. Every 2-4 days
C. Once or twice a week

2. How much does it hurt when you go poop?
A. Doesn't hurt at all!
B. Hurts a little bit
C. Hurts a lot

3. Do you feel constipated?
A. Nope!
B. A little bit
C. Yes

If you answered mostly...

A's: You probably don't have any stomach issues and are doing well.

B's: You might want to tell a parent to get checked out, so whatever is bothering you doesn't get worse.

C's: You will probably want to tell your parents, and get help with what is bothering you. Maybe try the bullet points. We don't want you to be in pain!

I recommend coming back to this one, just in case. It is important for us to tell what our bodies need, so we are not in pain.

Here are some things to try if you're not feeling well:

- Look up some recipes with dandelion root in them.

- Talk to your parents. They might not know about what is happening.

- Go to a therapist. It may sound like you need help, and you aren't strong, but that isn't true. You might need help, but you should still do what you need.

- Talk to your doctor. What do they say?

- Talk to your safe person.

Stress can be hard on your body, so make sure to take care of it. Remember to not hold your feelings or emotions in... let them out! You can do this by doing art, music, writing, or even talking! It is also so, so, so, soooo important to do a daily check-in with yourself. Ask yourself those check-in questions! Enduring our parents' divorces can put so much stress on our bodies, so we all need to make sure we are staying healthy.

7

I MISS U

Even though I'm mostly happy, I still sometimes feel like I am being pulled in between emotions like a tightrope. I go to one house, and when I finally get settled at that house, I have to go to the other one. But I also miss the other parent sometimes, too, and that is really hard.

For me, the summer schedule is really hard. It feels easier with vacations, but staying away from my mom for two weeks? Now, that is so hard. When I do have to stay away from her for too long, I start to cry. I try to text her a lot, and that helps. But the hardest part is not being able to hug or touch her.

This one week where I kept arguing with my dad. It was tiring, hard, and just not fun. All I wanted to do was be with my mom at that moment. I love my dad and I want him to know that, but sometimes I just need my mom.

When I miss one of my parents, I have learned a few tricks that might be helpful for you too. It's still hard and I still miss my mom. That part doesn't go away. But having some strategies helps. So here are a few that might help you too.

BEING MINDFUL

This meditation was inspired by my social studies teacher, Ms. Knutson. We did this one before a quiz, and it helped me a lot. Remember to read the whole thing before starting or listen to the track.

First, start by gently closing your eyes. Now, imagine your favorite place to be: home, the beach, your favorite creek, a hike, or maybe even simply in someone's arms. Now imagine this place. What does it feel like to be here? What can you smell? Can you taste anything? What about what you see? What do you hear?

Now, take a moment to be in this place. How does it make you feel? Calm? Happy?

Now slowly open your eyes and carry that feeling—that place—with you the rest of the day.

If you are stressed, or even mad or sad, it can be a little harder to check in with your whole body. This meditation hopefully helped you relax and notice how you are really feeling. Whenever I do this, even if I don't think it's working, I always feel better after taking a break.

Now you can journal about how you feel after doing this mindfulness exercise.

_____

_____

_____

_____

CREATIVE HUGS

Staying connected with the parent you won't get to see for a few days is really important. I was brainstorming ideas for this chapter with one of my friends, and she came up with the idea to leave "hugs" for the parent you won't get to see for a few days.

This is a crafty project, so if you are not a fan of that, you can do it your own way. Maybe just leave a handwritten note, send an email if you can email, or even send a text message if you have access to a phone. But if you want to be creative, try this project. All you need is creativity and love.

INSTRUCTIONS:

1. Get a piece of paper and cut a medium-sized rectangle or any shape you want. It could be a heart, a star, etc.

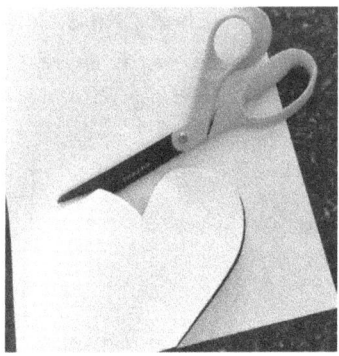

2. Write a message you want to give to this parent. Some examples are: "I love you" or "I miss you." You could even do an inside joke! Just try to make it meaningful.

3. Next is the fun part. Get out your tape, markers, crayons, colored pencils, and glitter glue, because it's time to get decorating! And have some fun with it!

4. Color your hug with color and glitter. Make sure you put some love and thought into it.

5. Add your finishing details, and leave it somewhere that parent looks every day. Maybe under their laptop, on their bedside, near their glasses. That way, you know that they have a part of you; your hugs might help for however long you are away from that parent.

Once you are done with this activity, and you are back with the parent, tell them about it. Maybe they could do it, too! That way, you will have a little bit of them, and they will have a little bit of you.

When you miss a parent, it can be hard. But you could also think of the situation as a sleepover, or even count down the days. Your parents want you to be happy, so try to enjoy yourself.

You could also keep a notebook that you carry back and forth. For example, you could have one where you keep up with everything you do when you aren't with your parent, and they can keep one where she notes the things that happened at the house while you were with your other parent. Then, you could switch notebooks so that neither of you feels like you are missing out.

The hardest part of the divorce is missing someone you love. It's just hard. The hardest part was realizing I couldn't do anything about it—ever. I had to develop strategies and they work. I hope they help you when you are missing one of your parents.

8

A NEW STEP

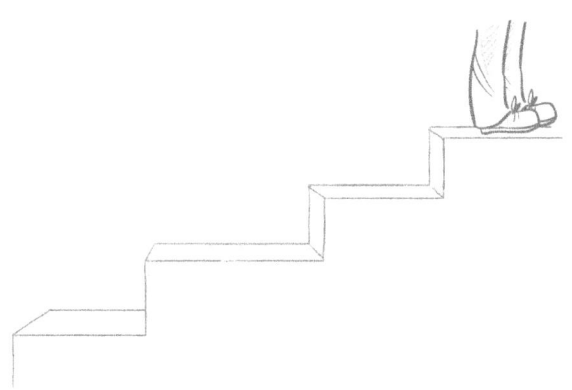

Now we're getting a little bit deeper into divorce. Not just the "I miss you" or "I want you to be together" but the "I have a stepmom" and "Why do things have to keep on getting more complicated and harder?" This chapter is about having a stepparent and helping you see both sides. If you do have one or are about to have one, don't worry too much about it. Just remember that whatever happens, happens. Whatever is, is. Let it be.

I know that when my dad got married, it was fun but also different and somewhat challenging. But I do remember the night he proposed. I had a mixture of feelings, and it was all coming at once. When they got married, she moved into the house. She also decorated it and stuff like that.

With new changes, you have to make sure to check in with yourself and look at both sides. I am happy my dad is happy and is in love, it's nice to see your parents happy. But I would be lying if I didn't say it was also really hard and sometimes it's confusing. My dad wants us to have a new family at his house, but it's hard because I also have my mom, and nothing can replace my mom even though I am happy my dad is happy.

So, what exactly does it mean to see both sides?

I was talking to one of my safe people, who is also a close family friend, and one of my best friends' mom. Her name is Jenny. One day, I was talking to Jenny about having a stepparent. Jenny told me she was a stepmom too, and that's a hard job. Jenny is a stepmom to her husband's two older children, who are super nice too. Jenny married Laurent and had Luly and Beatrice, but she was still a stepmom.

She told me that being a stepparent is hard because you are not the parent, and the only role of a stepparent is to be positive. Jenny said she never acted like the parent or "the mom" to her stepchildren—just another person who loved them and offered supportive and positive energy into the relationship.

It helped to hear how Jenny saw her job as a stepparent. It helped to know that as a stepparent, she didn't want to replace other the parent, but she was just an extra person who loved the children.

As a kid, it's confusing because you already have one dad and one mom. So when a new step is introduced, it feels different and weird. I didn't want to hurt my mom's feelings or my dad's feelings about having a stepparent. I worried a lot about how the other parent was feeling. It was hard. After I talked about this with some of my safe people, it helped.

My stepmom shares her stories from her childhood too. It helps to get to know her better, and her baby (my half-brother).

It can still help you find both sides. Talk to both parents about how you are feeling. One thing is for sure. You should not hold your feelings inside. It's okay to feel whatever you feel. So, if you feel like you're having a hard time with a new situation, and everything is out of your control, try to see both sides

My advice to anyone in a similar situation is to talk to your safe people about your feelings. It's okay to feel confused and sad and happy. Sometimes I feel all of them. At first, I felt sad that my mom wasn't remarried because I didn't want her to be alone. But I talked to my mom about this. She told me she was never alone because our hearts are always connected.

She also told me that she wanted me to feel happy, loved, and safe at my dad's house. She said the more people who love me the better. She reminded me that my dad will always be my dad—100 percent, nobody else can do that important job, and the same goes for my mom. Hearing both sides helped me feel better because before I talked to my safe people, I just held in all my feelings, thinking I knew what my parents were feeling.

BOX BREATHING

My school counselor, Ms. Roman, gave me this meditation: box breathing. Box breathing can help your mind relax, lower your stress levels, activate your parasympathetic nervous system, and so much more. This mindfulness is also short, so it is easier to memorize.

Try to do this exercise if you are stressed about a test or need a break. Also, you don't need to do this right away. Take your time finding a quiet room and a comfortable position to be in.

Steps:

1. Inhale to the count of 4.

2. Hold your breath to the count of 4.

3. Exhale to count of 4.

4. Hold the break to the count of 4.

Try to do at least four cycles of this meditation. If you want, you can even try to change it from four to eight, or any number!

Now take a few minutes after this exercise and journal how you feel:

_____

_____

_____

_____

LISTING THE PROS AND CONS

Having a stepparent can be hard, but there are some fun parts to it. So, if you are trying to comprehend everything, and it is getting to be too much for you, try to make a pros and cons list. Try to fill all of the spots out.

Cons:

1._____

2._____

3._____

4._____

5._____

6._____

7._____

8._____

9._____

10._____

Pros:

1._____

2._____

3._____

4._____

5._____

6._____

7._____

8._____

9._____

10._____

I know this might sound weird, but try to look at the cons list. How can you make it so that all of these cons can be a pro? If you can't think of anything, try to reflect on the pros list. Why are these important to you?

Another thing you can do is write in your journal about the cons. How are they affecting you? What could you do to make them pros?

I am still learning how to turn the cons into pros. I mentioned how the house changed when my stepmom moved into my dad's house. She also brought her dog (our dog now), but that dog didn't get along with one of our dogs, so we had to get rid of our dog to make room for her dog. That was hard, but later we got a new dog that we all named together. My dad's house is different from my mom's house, and I have to make weekly adjustments when I bounce back and forth between their houses.

Having a new step is a huge change. It's not easy for anyone, but you will get through it, even when you think you won't. If you have a half-sibling, this might work for you too. It can be hard to know how to feel before you meet your half-sibling. But once they're in your world, they can become close like your biological siblings.

I know I still have much to learn about how to navigate this new situation, but having the tools listed above and my safe people have really helped, and it's okay that I don't know all of the changes as long as I know that I am loved.

CONCLUSION

A GAME OF LEAPFROG

What does this all mean? If you have been asking yourself this question throughout the book, the answer is that no matter what anyone says and no matter what they tell you to feel, divorce is *hard*. It is hard for the parents, it is hard for you, and it is not fun. Who wants to feel like they are playing a constant game of leapfrog from house to house or even only seeing the other parent once a week?

I really hope this book helps you feel more understood and gives you the tools you need to deal with this. If you haven't yet, try to talk to your parents about what you need to thrive at your houses. Because you deserve to thrive and not feel like you are doing an endless relay race with just yourself.

My hope is not for this to be a best-seller but to help you, whoever is reading this book, whether you or someone else.

Please remember this is *not* the only source of help you can get. You should try to work with your safe person and use other tools that you learned about in this book and so many others too.

APPENDIX

INTRODUCTION
Owenby Law, P.A. "Statistics: Children and Divorce." *Owenby Law, P.A.*, October 11, 2018.
https://www.owenbylaw.com/blog/2018/october/statistics-children-divorce/.

CHAPTER 1: DIVORCE
Lazic, Marija. "13 Saddening Children of Divorce Statistics for 2022. *LegalJobs*, January 4, 2021.
https://legaljobs.io/blog/children-of-divorce-statistics/.

CHAPTER 2: HOW TO FIND YOUR SAFE PERSON
Bilotta, Larry. "18 Shocking Children and Divorce Statistics." *Marriage Success Secrets.* Accessed May 24, 2022.
http://www.marriage-success-secrets.com/statistics-about-children-and-divorce.html.

CHAPTER 4: NOT YOUR FAULT
Bay Atlantic University. "What Is a Kinesthetic Learner?" *Bay Atlantic University*, January 25, 2022.
https://bau.edu/blog/kinesthetic-learner/.

Silvi, Saxena. "Havening: What It Is and How It Works." *LegalJobs*, February 4, 2022.
https://www.choosingtherapy.com/havening/.

Study.com. "Auditory Learners: Definition and Characteristics." *Study.com*, September 23, 2017.
https://study.com/academy/lesson/auditory-learners-definition-characteristics.html.

Trussell, Jessica. "Activities for Helping Children Deal with Divorce." *The University of Missouri*, Accessed May 29, 2022.
https://extension.missouri.edu/publications/gh6602.

CHAPTER 5: PHYSICAL SYMPTOMS OF SEPARATION

Bourbeau, Lise. *Your Body's Telling You: Love Yourself!* St-Jérôme, QC: Editions E. T. C., 2014.

Gallagher, Kimberly. *Herb Fairies Book Thirteen: Healing the Heart of the Forest.* Seattle: LearningHerbs, 2015.

ACKNOWLEDGMENTS

Oh my gosh, I am so grateful for *everyone* who helped me! This was such a fun amazing process, and even though it was challenging sometimes, so many people helped me through it.

I first want to thank my mom for helping me so much and loving me twenty-four-seven. I want to thank my dad for being there and supporting me along the way. I want to thank all of my friends for being *so amazing* and helping me no matter what, and thank you, Bridget, for giving me the idea for my favorite activity.

I also want to thank the people who made this book happen. Angela Ivy, thank you so much for making this so much less confusing. Thank you, Whitney McGruder, for being so nice to me and helping me finish.

Thank you to my safe people, Ms. Roman, Liz, Ms. Bloomston, Ms. Tamer, Ms. Wood, and Ms. Harris. And I cannot forget *all* of my teachers who have been so incredible and amazing to me. If I listed everyone I wanted to thank, this book would go on and on and on... so thank you to everyone who helped me with this incredible process. You are the best!

Thank you to my **OVER THE MOON FANS**: Nana and Papa Roberts a.k.a. Marsha and Joel Roberts, Jennifer Chase and Laurent Poole, Luly and Beatrice Poole

Thank you to my **SUPER BIG FANS**: Stephen Kahn and Sue Ellen Webb, Jamie, Pete, Zoe, Jacob and Charlotte Sunenshine

Thank you to my **HUGE SUPPORT FANS**: Samantha, Jonathan, Noah, Leah and Micah Major, Michael Goldstein and Paula Wagner, Marilyn Fransway, Gigi Fransway, Brooke and Harlow Levy

Thank you to my **SUPER DUPER SUPPORT FANS**: Julie Goggin, Alison Betts, The Gorlin Family (Gwen, Andy, Bridget, and George), The Mikalsky Family (Rachel, Michael, Grace, Alex, and Charlotte), The Stein Family (Sadie, Asher, Misha, and Talia), Stephanie Coker, Jessica, Rocco and Max Matosian, The Patil Family (Neelu, Avi, Jyothi, Ari, and Isha) The Rishi Family, Flo Eckstein, Elizabeth Tomko

Thank you for all of my AMAZING supporters: Johanna and Mira Baraff, Stacey Rosenthal, Alyssa Levin, Cassie Mills, Sara Strouts, Julie Weinstein, Carrie Bloomston, Julie Hymovich, Rachel Seymour Rhonda George, Debra Wood, Shannon Stringer Eric Koester, Marilyn Urdang, Mara Kotansky, Shannon Burke, Andria Tazioli and Nora Smith, Carla Belsher, Kelly Bishop, Susie Hair, Amy Herman, Julie Tamer, Nichole Dawson, Maria Roman, Larry Swanson

I also want to thank the entire team at New Degree Press for providing me the opportunity to publish this book. Thank you. I would also like to thank Eric Koester for being excited about publishing a book by a twelve-year-old kid.